Pebble® Plus

Dance, Dance, Dance

Jazz Dancing

by Kathryn Clay

Consulting editor: Gail Saunders-Smith, PhD

Content consultant: Heidi L. Schimpf,
Director of Programs and Services
Joy of Motion Dance Center
Washington, D.C.

CAPSTONE PRESS
a capstone imprint

Pebble Plus is published by Capstone Press,
151 Good Counsel Drive, P.O. Box 669, Mankato, Minnesota 56002.
www.capstonepress.com

092009
005618CGS10

Books published by Capstone Press are manufactured with paper
containing at least 10 percent post-consumer waste.

Library of Congress Cataloging-in-Publication Data
Clay, Kathryn.
    Jazz dancing / by Kathryn Clay.
    p. cm. — (Pebble plus. Dance, dance, dance)
    Includes bibliographical references and index.
    Summary: "Simple text and photographs present jazz dancing,
including simple steps" — Provided by publisher.
    ISBN 978-1-4296-4004-6 (library binding)
    1. Jazz dance. I. Title.
GV1784.C57 2010
793.3 — dc22   2009023384

Editorial Credits
Jennifer Besel, editor; Veronica Bianchini, designer;
    Marcie Spence, media researcher; Eric Manske, production specialist;
    Sarah Schuette, photo stylist; Marcy Morin, scheduler

Photo Credits
All photos by Capstone Studio/Karon Dubke

The Capstone Press Photo Studio thanks Dance Express in
Mankato, Minnesota, and The Dance Connection in Rosemount,
Minnesota, for their help with photo shoots for this book.

Note to Parents and Teachers

The Dance, Dance, Dance series supports national physical education standards and the
national standards for learning and teaching dance in the arts. This book describes and
illustrates jazz dancing. The images support early readers in understanding the text. The
repetition of words and phrases helps early readers learn new words. This book also introduces
early readers to subject-specific vocabulary words, which are defined in the Glossary section.
Early readers may need assistance to read some words and to use the Table of Contents,
Glossary, Read More, Internet Sites, and Index sections of the book.

Table of Contents

All about Jazz

Jump, turn, and shake!

You move your whole body

when you jazz dance.

Jazz dance is full of energy.

Dancers move to upbeat music.

Getting Ready

Jazz dancers wear jazz shoes.

Jazz shoes bend easily

to help dancers turn and jump.

Jazz dancers wear
leotards, tights,
and stretchy pants.
Stretchy clothes
let dancers move easily.

Dancers practice in studios.

Before practicing,

dancers warm up.

They stretch so they won't

hurt their muscles.

Sweet Steps

Jump into the air,

and curl your legs behind you.

This move is called a tuck.

Step one foot to the side.

Slide your other foot to meet it.

This move is called a chassé.

Say chassé:
sha-SAY

Stand on one leg,

and jump up high.

Kick your legs wide.

This move is called a leap.

Ready to Dance

It's recital time!

Dress up in a costume.

Show your jazz moves

on the stage.

Glossary

leotard — a tight piece of clothing worn by dancers

muscle — a body part that pulls on bones to make them move

recital — a show where people dance for others

studio — a room or building where a dancer practices

upbeat — quick and full of energy

Read More

Clay, Kathryn. *Tap Dancing*. Dance, Dance, Dance. Mankato, Minn.: Capstone Press, 2010.

Karapetkova, Holly. *Dance*. Sports for Sprouts. Vero Beach, Fla.: Rourke, 2010.

Schwaeber, Barbie Heit. *Alphabet of Dance*. Alphabet Books. Norwalk, Conn.: Soundprints, 2009.

Internet Sites

FactHound offers a safe, fun way to find Internet sites related to this book. All of the sites on FactHound have been researched by our staff.

Here's all you do:

Visit *www.facthound.com*

FactHound will fetch the best sites for you!

Index

Word Count: 138
Grade: 1
Early-Intervention Level: 13